EASY PIANO CLASSICS

97 Pieces for Early and Intermediate Players

Selected and edited by

Ronald Herder

DOVER PUBLICATIONS, INC.
Mineola, New York

Bibliographical Note

This Dover edition, first published in 1999, is a new compilation of music originally published in earlier Dover editions and other authoritative publications. This edition deletes editorial detail thought not to be original with the composer, and adds a glossary prepared specially for this publication.

The composer's name in a main heading is always followed by the name of his native country. Where two countries are named, the second refers to one closely identified with the composer's career.

International Standard Book Number: 0-486-40407-2

Manufactured in the United States of America
Dover Publications, Inc., 31 East 2nd Street, Mineola, N.Y. 11501

A NOTE TO THE PLAYER

To paraphrase my note to Dover's *Sonatinas and Easy Piano Sonatas,* "easy" is a deceptive description we give to some pieces, perhaps not strictly true all of the time. While we've favored finger-friendly passagework and the less complicated keys in this collection of "easy piano classics," our range of music gently pushes the envelope of "easy." On one end is Mozart's lightweight *Minuet in F* (composed, incredibly, in his kindergarten years); at the other, the handful of mighty chords in Mussorgsky's imposing *Promenade*—a wide but accessible technical range that spans the years from "early" to "intermediate," whatever those inexact terms have come to mean to us.

"Easy" does not mean "casual." There is nothing we should treat halfheartedly, for example, in Clementi's charming, ultrafamiliar *Sonatina in C*— to name but one "easy" piece among many. Even a variant of a simple scale demands respect, careful preparation and a musical approach. A good musician approaches every piece of music with thoughtful care, no matter what its technical level may be.

The music in this book originated in early publications prepared by a variety of editors. It is no surprise that no two of them saw eye to eye on the way a piece of music should be fingered, pedaled or otherwise prepared for the pianist. Some favored no fingerings at all, or sparse fingerings, or a fingering marked on every note in every bar! The same wild variety applied to markings for dynamics and for pedalings—more often than not overwhelming the composer's straightforward notation and uncluttered manuscript.

By deleting much of this detail, offering the player a cleaner page, we have chosen to return to basics wherever possible, leaving all musical—and editorial—matters up to the player and, for many fortunate pianists of all ages, his or her teacher.

Ronald Herder
New York, 1999

CONTENTS

ALKAN, CHARLES-VALENTIN
The Dying   1
(from *The Months*, Op. 74)

BACH, CARL PHILIPP EMANUEL
Rondo espressivo   4
Minuets   6
Nos. 1 & 2: D major / B minor
Nos. 3 & 4: C major / C minor
Nos. 5 & 6: F major / F minor
Solfeggietto   10

BACH, JOHANN SEBASTIAN
Prelude in C major   12
(No. 1 from *The Well-Tempered Clavier*, Book I)
Adagio in C minor   14
Musette in D major   15
Two Minuets   16
(from *The Little Notebook for Anna Magdalena Bach*)
Invention in D minor   18

BEETHOVEN, LUDWIG VAN
Sonatina in G major   20
I. Moderato
II. *Romanze*
Minuet in G major   22
Bagatelle: "Für Elise"   23
Variations on a Swiss Song   27
Bagatelle in D major (Op. 33, No. 6)   30

BRAHMS, JOHANNES
Waltzes (Op. 39)   32
No. 5 in E major
No. 8 in B-flat major
No. 9 in D minor
No. 15 in A major
No. 16 in D minor

BUXTEHUDE, DIETRICH
Sarabande and Gigue   36
(from *Suite XII in E minor*)

CHOPIN, FRÉDÉRIC
Préludes (Op. 28)   38
No. 6 in B minor
No. 7 in A major
No. 20 in C minor
Nocturne in G minor (Op. 37, No. 1)   40
Mazurka in G minor (Op. 67, No. 2)   44
Mazurka in F major (Op. 68, No. 3)   46

CLARKE, JEREMIAH
Trumpet Tune   48

CLEMENTI, MUZIO
Sonatina in C major (Op. 36, No. 1)   49
I. Spiritoso
II. Andante
III. Vivace
Sonatina in G major (Op. 36, No. 2)   52
I. Allegretto
II. Allegretto
III. Allegro

DANDRIEU, JEAN-FRANÇOIS
The Eager Young Girl   56

DAQUIN, LOUIS-CLAUDE
The Tuneful Girl: *Rondeau*   58

DEBUSSY, CLAUDE
Jimbo's Lullaby   62
(from *Children's Corner*)

DELIBES, LÉO
Passepied   66
(from *Six Dance Tunes in Olden Style*)

DUSSEK, JAN LADISLAV
Sonatina in E-flat major (Op. 19/20, No. 6)   70
I. Allegro
II. *Rondo:* Allegretto

DVOŘÁK, ANTONÍN
Silhouette in D-flat major (Op. 8, No. 2)   77

FRANCK, CÉSAR
A Doll's Laments   78
Slow Dance   80

GLUCK, CHRISTOPH WILLIBALD
Air de Ballet   82
(from *Orfeo ed Euridice*)

GOSSEC, FRANÇOIS-JOSEPH
Gavotte   83

GRIEG, EDVARD
Gjendine's Lullaby (Op. 66, No. 19)   87
Waltz in A minor (Op. 12, No. 2)   88
Watchman's Song (Op. 12, No. 3)   90
Grandmother's Minuet (Op. 68, No. 2)   92

HANDEL, GEORGE FRIDERIC
Largo   96
(from *Serse*)
Sarabande in D minor   98

HAYDN, JOSEPH
Sonata in C major (Hob. 35)   99
First movement

JOPLIN, SCOTT
Bethena: A Concert Waltz   105

LISZT, FRANZ
Consolation in E major   111
Pater Noster   112
(from *Poetic and Religious Harmonies*)
Nuages Gris   114

LULLY, JEAN-BAPTISTE
Tender Melody   116

MACDOWELL, EDWARD
To a Wild Rose   118
From an Indian Lodge   120
A Deserted Farm   122
(all from *Woodland Sketches,* Op. 51)

MASSENET, JULES
Élégie (Op. 10, No. 5)   124

MENDELSSOHN, FELIX
Venetian Gondola Song (Op. 30, No. 6)   126
Little Piece (Op. 72, No. 1)   128

MOZART, WOLFGANG AMADEUS
Allegro in B-flat major   129
Four Early Minuets   130
Minuet in D major (K94)   133
Minuet in D major (K355)   134
Two German Dances   136

MUSSORGSKY, MODEST
Promenade   138
(from *Pictures at an Exhibition*)

PURCELL, HENRY
Lilliburlero: A New Irish Tune   140
Minuet in A minor   141
Air in D minor   142
Hornpipe in E minor   143

RAMEAU, JEAN-PHILIPPE
Tambourin   144

SCARLATTI, DOMENICO
Sonata in D minor (Gavotta)   146

SCHUBERT, FRANZ
Eight Ländler (D378)   148

SCHUMANN, ROBERT
Little Study   152
The Happy Farmer   154
(both from *Album for the Young,* Op. 68)
Träumerei   155
Child Falling Asleep   156
(both from *Scenes from Childhood,* Op. 15)

SCRIABIN, ALEXANDER
Prelude (Op. 16, No. 3)   158
Prelude (Op. 16, No. 4)   160

TCHAIKOVSKY, PETER ILYITCH
Morning Prayer   161
Marches of the Wooden Soldiers   162
German Song   163
In Church   164
The Hurdy-Gurdy   165
(all from *Album for the Young,* Op. 39)

ALPHABETICAL LIST OF TITLES

A

Adagio (J. S. Bach)   14
Air (Purcell)   142
Air de Ballet (Gluck)   82
Allegro (Mozart)   129

B

Bagatelle: "Für Elise" (Beethoven)   23
Bagatelle in D major (Beethoven)   30
Bethena (Joplin)   105

C

Child Falling Asleep (Schumann)   156
Consolation in E major (Liszt)   111

D

Deserted Farm, A (MacDowell)   122
Doll's Laments, A (Franck)   78
Dying, The (Alkan)   1

E

Eager Young Girl, The (Dandrieu)   56
Élégie (Massenet)   124

F

From an Indian Lodge (MacDowell)   120
"Für Elise" (see *Bagatelle*)

G

Gavotta (see *Sonata by Scarlatti*)
Gavotte (Gossec)   83
German Dances (Mozart)   136, 137
German Song (Tchaikovsky)   163
Gigue (Buxtehude)   36
Gjendine's Lullaby (Grieg)   87
Grandmother's Minuet (Grieg)   92

H

Happy Farmer, The (Schumann)   154
Hornpipe (Purcell)   143
Hurdy-Gurdy, The (Tchaikovsky)   165

I

In Church (Tchaikovsky)   164
Invention in D minor (J. S. Bach)   18

J

Jimbo's Lullaby (Debussy)   62

L

Ländler (Schubert)   148–151
Largo (Handel)   96
Lilliburlero (Purcell)   140
Little Piece (Mendelssohn)   128
Little Study (Schumann)   152

M

Marches of the Wooden Soldiers (Tchaikovsky)   162
Mazurka in F major (Chopin)   46
Mazurka in G minor (Chopin)   44
Minuets
    by C. P. E. Bach   6–9
    by J. S. Bach   16, 17
    by Beethoven   22
    by Mozart   130–135
    by Purcell   141
Morning Prayer (Tchaikovsky)   161
Musette (J. S. Bach)   15

N

Nocturne (Chopin)   40
Nuages Gris (Liszt)   114

P

Passepied (Delibes)   66
Pater Noster (Liszt)   112
Preludes
    by J. S. Bach   12
    by Chopin   38, 39
    by Scriabin   158, 160
Promenade (Mussorgsky)   138

R

Rondo espressivo (C. P. E. Bach)   4

S

Sarabandes
   by Buxtehude   36
   by Handel   98
Silhouette (Dvořák)   77
Slow Dance (Franck)   80
Solfeggietto (C. P. E. Bach)   10
Sonatas
   by Haydn   99
   by Scarlatti   146
Sonatinas
   by Beethoven   20
   by Clementi   49, 52
   by Dussek   70

T

Tambourin (Rameau)   144
Tender Melody (Lully)   116
To a Wild Rose (MacDowell)   118
Träumerei (Schumann)   155
Trumpet Tune (Clarke)   48
Tuneful Girl, The (Daquin)   58

V

Variations on a Swiss Song (Beethoven)   27
Venetian Gondola Song (Mendelssohn)   126

W

Waltzes
   by Brahms   32–35
   by Grieg   88
Watchman's Song (Grieg)   90

GLOSSARY

adagio (sostenuto), very slow (and sustained)

al fine, to the end

allarg[ando], slowing down

allegretto, moderately fast

    grazioso, . . . with a graceful lilt

    nel modo russico, . . . in Russian style

    semplice, . . . in a simple manner

    tranquillo, . . . and tranquilly

allegro, fast

    con brio, . . . with vigor and spirit

    giusto, . . . and in strict time

    moderato, moderately fast

    (ma) non troppo, (but) not too fast

    vivace, . . . and lively

andante, walking tempo

    cantabile, . . . in a songful manner

    con moto, moving along

    grazioso, . . . with a graceful lilt

    sostenuto, . . . and sustained

andantino, slightly faster than a walking tempo

animé / animato, animated, lively

assez, rather, somewhat

assez modéré, in a rather moderate tempo

a tempo [primo / I⁰], return to the first speed

calando, becoming softer, and usually slowing down

cantabile, in a lyrical manner

cantando, songful

coda, "tailpiece," end (of the music)

con moto, with motion, quick

con spirito, spiritedly

con una certa espressione parlante,
    played in the manner of a spoken expression

cresc[endo], getting louder

da capo al fine, return to the beginning of the music,
    then play up to the place marked *"fine"* (end)

dim[inuendo], becoming softer

dolce / doux, gentle, sweet

dolcissimo, extremely gentle, sweet

doux et un peu gauche, gentle and a bit clumsy

e / et, and

espr[essivo], expressively

fine, end (of the music)

frisch und munter, bright and gay

grazioso, graziosamente, graceful(ly)

in tempo, resume the first speed

Ländler, an Austrian country dance
    (predecessor of the waltz)

largo, slow, stately

legatissimo, extremely smooth, connected

legato, smooth, connected

leggierissimo, extremely lightly

legg., leggiero / légèrement, lightly

lento, slow

    assai, rather slow

    (ma) non troppo, . . . (but) not too much so

    sostenuto, . . . and sustained

les 2 Ped[ales], [for a piano with three pedals]
    sustain the low note with the *sostenuto* pedal
    while playing the rest of the passage

maggiore, in the major key

main droite / m.d., right hand

main gauche / m.g., left hand

mancando, dying away

marcato / marqué, marked, accented

men. da capo, return to the beginning of the minuet

moderato, at a moderate speed

molto, very

molto andante e semplice, very simply
    in a clear *andante* tempo

molto legato, played in an extremely smooth manner

molto più lento capriccio, somewhat slow,
 but played very freely
molto vivace, very fast and lively
morendo (jusqu'à la fin), dying away
 (until the end of the music)
mosso, with motion
musette, a pastoral dance featuring a sustained drone
 (imitating the French bagpipe called "musette")

perdendosi, dying away in speed and volume
più, more
  forte, louder
  lento, slower
  mosso, faster
  vivo, livelier
poco, a little, somewhat
  allargando, somewhat broadened in tempo
  moto, with a little motion (movement)
  più, a little more
  più vivo, a little livelier
  rinf[orzando], slightly accented
  rit[ardando], slowing down a little
  riten[uto], held back a little
  rubato, with some flexible give-and-take
   in the speed of the beat
   [see main listing for *rubato*]
  sostenuto, somewhat sustained
poco a poco, little by little
presto, very fast

quasi lento (e smorzando), almost slow
 (and fading away)
quasi recitativo, somewhat in the manner
 of a recitative

rall[entando], slowing down
retenu, held back
rit[ardando], holding back (gradual tempo change)
riten[uto], held back (immediate tempo change)

rubato, most typically, a flexible give-and-take in the
 flow of a melodic line, compared to an accompani-
 ment held in fairly strict tempo (as in a Chopin waltz)

sans retarder, without slowing down
scherzando, lightly, playfully
scherzoso, playful, jesting
sempre, always
senza, without
smorz[ando], fading away in tempo and volume
solfeggietto, a small study
sost[enuto], sustained
sotto voce, subdued (literally, "under the voice")
spiritoso, spirited
stretto, gathering force and speed
string[endo], hurrying

tempo, time, speed of the beat
  di marcia, in march tempo
  di valse, in waltz tempo
  primo (I°), first (original) tempo
  rubato [see main listing for *rubato*]
ten[uto], held, sustained
thema, theme
toujours, always
tranquillo, tranquil
tremolando, literally "trembling":
 a rapid alternation of two or more pitches
 to produce a continuously resonating sound,
 usually used as a harmonic background
tristamente, sadly

un peu, a little
  en dehors, somewhat emphasized, brought out
  plus mouvementé, with a little more motion
un poco mosso, a little more
un poco rit[ardando], slightly held back
un poco stretto, slightly rushing ahead

valse, waltz
vif, brisk
vivace, vivacious, lively
vivo, quick

The Dying

(representing November from *The Months*, Op. 74, *ca.* 1872)

Charles-Valentin Alkan
(France, 1813–1888)

Rondo espressivo

Carl Philipp Emanuel Bach
(Germany, 1714–1788)

Andante sostenuto

p cantabile

Six Minuets

Carl Philipp Emanuel Bach

7

8

Solfeggietto

Carl Philipp Emanuel Bach

Allegro

Prelude in C major

(No. 1 from *The Well-Tempered Clavier*, Book I, 1722)

Johann Sebastian Bach
(Germany, 1685–1750)

Adagio in C minor

Johann Sebastian Bach

Musette in D major

[Allegro]

Johann Sebastian Bach

[poco rit.]

Two Minuets

(from *The Little Notebook for Anna Magdalena Bach, ca. 1722*)

Johann Sebastian Bach

I

II

[Andante grazioso]

Invention in D minor

(No. 4 of *Fifteen [Two-part] Inventions*, 1723)

Johann Sebastian Bach

Sonatina in G major

(No. 2 of *Three Easy Sonatinas*)

Ludwig van Beethoven
(Germany & Austria, 1770–1827)

Romanze.

Minuet in G major

(ca. 1795)

Ludwig van Beethoven

Men. da capo.

Bagatelle: "Für Elise"

(1808)

Ludwig van Beethoven

Poco moto

Variations on a Swiss Song

(before 1793)

Ludwig van Beethoven

Thema
Andante con moto

Bagatelle in D major

(No. 6 of *Seven Bagatelles*, Op. 33, 1801–2)

Ludwig van Beethoven

Allegretto, quasi Andante
Con una certa espressione parlante

Five Waltzes

(Nos. 5, 8, 9, 15 & 16 from *Waltzes*, Op. 39, 1865)

Johannes Brahms
(Germany & Austria, 1833–1897)

34

Sarabande and Gigue

(from *Suite XII in E minor*)

Dietrich Buxtehude
(Germany *or* Denmark, *ca.* 1637–1707)

Sarabande

Gigue

Prélude in B minor

(No. 6 of *24 Préludes,* Op. 28, 1836–9)

Frédéric Chopin
(Poland & France, 1810–1849)

Prélude in A major

(No. 7 of *24 Préludes*, Op. 28)

Frédéric Chopin

Prélude in C minor

(No. 20 of *24 Préludes*, Op. 28)

Frédéric Chopin

Nocturne in G minor

(No. 1 of *Two Nocturnes*, Op. 37, 1838)

Frédéric Chopin

Mazurka in G minor

(No. 2 of *Four Mazurkas*, Op. 67, 1849)

Frédéric Chopin

Mazurka in F major

(No. 3 of *Four Mazurkas,* Op. 68, 1829)

Allegro, ma non troppo.

Frédéric Chopin

Trumpet Tune

Con spirito

Jeremiah Clarke
(England, *ca.* 1674–1707)

Sonatina in C major

(No. 1 of *Six Progressive Pianoforte Sonatinas*, Op. 36, 1797)

Muzio Clementi
(Italy, 1752–1832)

Spiritoso.

Sonatina in G major

(No. 2 of *Six Sonatinas,* Op. 36)

Muzio Clementi

Allegretto.

54

Allegro.

The Eager Young Girl

L'empressée

Jean-François Dandrieu
(France, *ca.* 1682–1738)

Briskly and lightly
(*Vif et légèrement*)

The Tuneful Girl

La mélodieuse: Rondeau

Louis-Claude Daquin
(France, ca. 1694–1772)

COUPLET II

Jimbo's Lullaby

(No. 2 from the suite *Children's Corner*, 1906–8)

Claude Debussy
(France, 1862–1918)

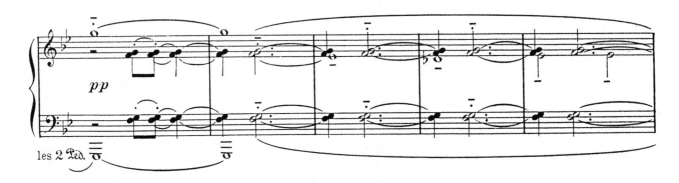

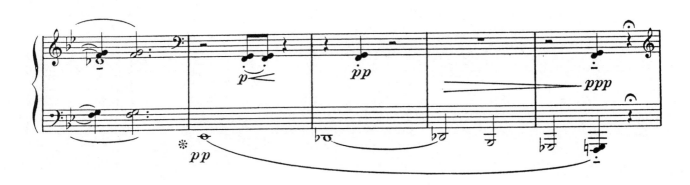

Passepied

(from *Le roi s'amuse: Six airs de danse dans le style ancien*, 1882)

[The King at Play: Six Dance Tunes in Olden Style]

Léo Delibes
(France, 1836–1891)

Sonatina in E-flat major

(No. 6 of *Six Sonatinas*, 1793; published as both Op. 19 & 20)

Transcribed by the composer from the work for piano and flute or violin

Jan Ladislav Dussek
(Bohemia & France, 1760–1812)

RONDO.
Allegretto.

Silhouette in D-flat major

(No. 2 of twelve *Silhouettes,* Op. 8, 1879)

Antonín Dvořák
(Czechoslovakia, 1841–1904)

Audantino.

A Doll's Laments

Les plaintes d'une poupée

(1865)

César Franck
(Belgium & France, 1822–1890)

Slow Dance

Danse lente

(1885)

César Franck

Air de Ballet

(from the opera *Orfeo ed Euridice*, 1762)

Christoph Willibald Gluck
(Germany & Austria, 1714–1787)

Gavotte

(from the opera *Rosine*, 1786)

François-Joseph Gossec
(Netherlands & France, 1734–1829)

84

COUPLET II

Gjendine's Lullaby

(No. 19 from *Norwegian Folk Tunes,* Op. 66, 1896)

Edvard Grieg
(Norway, 1843–1907)

Waltz in A minor

(No. 2 from *Lyric Pieces*, Op. 12, 1866)

Edvard Grieg

Allegro moderato.

Watchman's Song

(No. 3 from *Lyric Pieces*, Op. 12, 1867)

Composed after attending a performance of Shakespeare's Macbeth

Edvard Grieg

Grandmother's Minuet

(No. 2 from *Lyric Pieces*, Op. 68, 1899)

Edvard Grieg

Tempo I.

Largo

(arranged from the opera *Serse*, 1738)

George Frideric Handel
(Germany & England, 1685–1759)

Sarabande in D minor

(from the *Suite in D minor, ca.* 1720)

George Frideric Handel

Sonata in C major

Sonata No. 35 in the Hoboken catalog

(First movement) (1780)

Joseph Haydn
(Austria, 1732–1809)

Bethena

A Concert Waltz

(1905)

Scott Joplin
(United States, 1868–1917)

108

Consolation in E major

(No. 1 of six *Consolations*, 1849–50)

Franz Liszt
(Hungary & Germany, 1811–1886)

Pater Noster

Our Father

(No. 5 of *Harmonies poétiques et religieuses,* before 1852)

[Poetic and Religious Harmonies]

Transcribed by the composer from the original for voices and organ, 1848

Franz Liszt

Nuages Gris

Somber Clouds

(1881)

Franz Liszt

sempre legato

rallent.

p

Ped. ✻ Ped. ✻

Tender Melody

Air Tendre

Jean-Baptiste Lully
(Italy & France, 1632–1687)

To a Wild Rose

(No. 1 of ten *Woodland Sketches,* Op. 51, 1896)

Edward MacDowell
(United States, 1860–1908)

With simple tenderness.

slightly marked

From an Indian Lodge

(No. 5 of *Woodland Sketches*, Op. 51)

Edward MacDowell

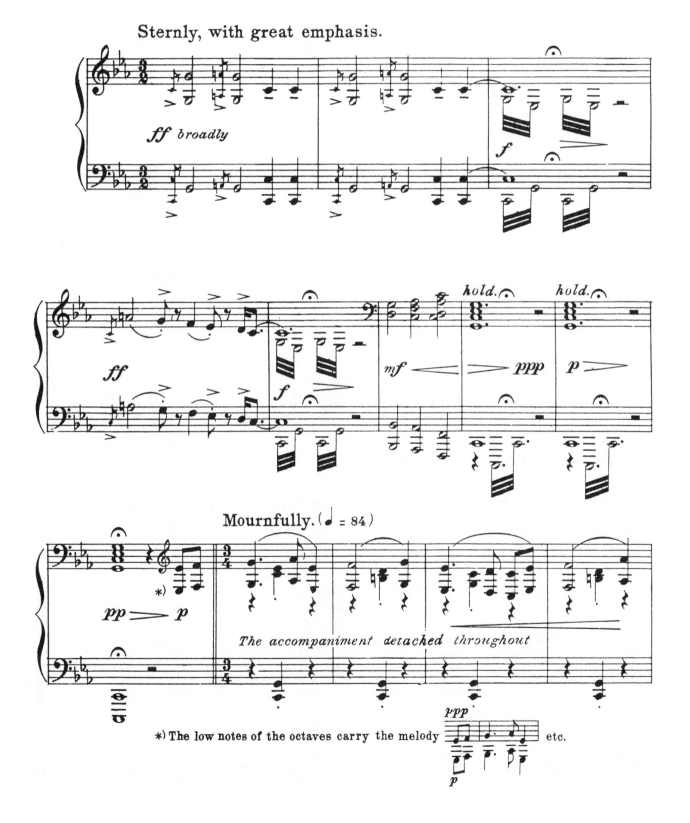

*) The low notes of the octaves carry the melody

*) The upper notes of the octaves carry the melody   etc.

A Deserted Farm

(No. 8 of *Woodland Sketches*, Op. 51)

Edward MacDowell

Élégie

(originally, "Mélodie": No. 5 of *Ten Characteristic Pieces,* Op. 10, 1866)

Jules Massenet
(France, 1842–1912)

Lento, ma non troppo

Venetian Gondola Song

(No. 6 of six *Songs without Words,* Op. 30, 1833)

Felix Mendelssohn
(Germany, 1809–1847)

Little Piece

(No. 1 of six *Children's Pieces*, Op. 72, 1847)

Felix Mendelssohn

Allegro non troppo.

Allegro in B-flat major

(1762)

Wolfgang Amadeus Mozart
(Austria, 1756–1791)

Four Early Minuets

(1761–2)

I

Wolfgang Amadeus Mozart

Menuetto da Capo al Fine.

II

III

IV

Minuet in D major

(Köchel 94, 1769 / *later catalogued as K73h*)

Wolfgang Amadeus Mozart

Minuet in D major

(Köchel 355, *ca.* 1786 / *later catalogued as K576b*)

Wolfgang Amadeus Mozart

Two German Dances

Wolfgang Amadeus Mozart

I

Fine

Trio

da capo al Fine

II

Fine

Trio

da capo al Fine

Promenade

(from the suite *Pictures at an Exhibition*, 1874)

Modest Mussorgsky
(Russia, 1839–1881)

Allegro giusto, nel modo russico, poco sostenuto.

Lilliburlero

A New Irish Tune

(No. 646 in the Zimmermann catalog)

Henry Purcell
(England, 1659–1695)

Minuet in A minor

(Zimmermann No. 649)

Henry Purcell

Air in D minor

(incidental music for William Congreve's play *The Double-Dealer*, 1693)

Henry Purcell

Andante.

Hornpipe in E minor

(incidental music for William Congreve's play *The Old Bachelor*, 1693)

Henry Purcell

144

Tambourin

(from *Harpsichord Pieces*, 1724)

Jean-Philippe Rameau
(France, 1683–1764)

*a long, narrow drum from Provence

Sonata in D minor

Gavotta

(No. 58 in the Longo catalog)

Domenico Scarlatti
(Italy, 1685–1757)

Eight Ländler

(No. 378 in the Deutsch catalog)

(1816)

Franz Schubert
(Austria, 1797–1828)

Predecessor of the waltz, the *ländler* is a robust partnered folkdance in slow 3/4 time, originally performed on the village greens of 17th-century Austria. Individual *ländler* were often gathered together (as in this Schubert work) to form a kind of "ländler chain."

N° 7.

N° 8.

Little Study

(No. 14 from *Album for the Young*, Op. 68, 1848)

Robert Schumann
(Germany, 1810–1856)

Played lightly and very equally throughout

The Happy Farmer

(No. 10 from *Album for the Young*, Op. 68)

Robert Schumann

Frisch und munter *(bright and gay)*

Träumerei

Reverie

(No. 7 from *Scenes from Childhood,* Op. 15, 1838)

Robert Schumann

Moderato

Child Falling Asleep

(No. 12 from *Scenes from Childhood*, Op. 15)

Robert Schumann

Lento non troppo

Prelude

(No. 3 of *Five Preludes*, Op. 16, 1894–5)

Alexander Scriabin
(Russia, 1872–1915)

Andante cantabile

Prelude

(No. 4 of *Five Preludes*, Op. 16)

Alexander Scriabin

Morning Prayer

Prière de matin

(No. 1 from *Album for the Young,* Op. 39, 1878)

Peter Ilyitch Tchaikovsky
(Russia, 1840–1893)

Marches of the Wooden Soldiers

Marches des soldats de bois

(No. 5 from *Album for the Young*, Op. 39)

Peter Ilyitch Tchaikovsky

Tempo di Marcia.

German Song

Chanson allemande

(No. 17 from *Album for the Young*, Op. 39)

Peter Ilyitch Tchaikovsky

In Church

A l'église

(No. 23 from *Album for the Young*, Op. 39)

Peter Ilyitch Tchaikovsky

Largo.

The Hurdy-Gurdy

L'orgue de barbarie

(No. 24 from *Album for the Young*, Op. 39)

Peter Ilyitch Tchaikovsky

END OF EDITION